The Seasons Reside in the Trees

poems by

Taylor Tessa Lutz

Finishing Line Press
Georgetown, Kentucky

The Seasons Reside in the Trees

Copyright © 2018 by Taylor Tessa Lutz
ISBN 978-1-63534-711-1 First Edition
All rights reserved under International and Pan-American Copyright Conventions.
No part of this book may be reproduced in any manner whatsoever without written permission from the publisher, except in the case of brief quotations embodied in critical articles and reviews.

ACKNOWLEDGMENTS

I want to thank the teachers, mentors, and loved ones that have helped nurture me as an individual and my passion for writing. *The Seasons Reside in the Trees* grew from your support and love. I also gratefully acknowledge *The Paddock Review* for featuring my work and Finishing Line Press for allowing the words in this book a chance to blossom in the hearts of its readers.

Publisher: Leah Maines
Editor: Christen Kincaid
Cover Art: Taylor Tessa Lutz
Author Photo: Avery Bradney
Cover Design: Elizabeth Maines McCleavy

Printed in the USA on acid-free paper.
Order online: www.finishinglinepress.com
also available on amazon.com

Author inquiries and mail orders:
Finishing Line Press
P. O. Box 1626
Georgetown, Kentucky 40324
U. S. A.

Table of Contents

A Photograph of the Sun (Self-Portrait) 1
It's You 2
Love Poem that Ends in Apocalypse 4
Class Discussion 5
One Cannot Bargain for a True Gift 6
gravitational pull 8
A Elegy for the Baby Bird that Cared 9
haunted 11
The Nature of Our Wrongs 12
What Remains Between Us 14
I Hide It Surprisingly Well 15
The Poem without Forgiveness 16
Taking on the Sun 17
The Epoxy of Our Pasts 18
Hope is a Dammed Thing 19
We Would Be Aligned with the Universe Again 21
The Poem That Knows Something 22
Worlds Away 23
Just Keep Walking 24
The Nature of the Beast 25
writing at dawn 26
What I Want You to Know 27
The Seasons in the Trees 28

Letter from the Author:

I had a poetry professor tell me once that we do not write because we are expecting anyone else to read our work, we write because we have to. I wrote *The Seasons Reside in the Trees* in personal journal entries tucked secretly away, never expecting anyone to read them.

I wrote these poems because I needed a way to make sense of the events in my life that were happening. This collection of poems explores the complexity of relationships and the sentimentality in their disaster. These poems engage in the turmoil of trying to save loved ones from their own gravity of destruction, yet, discover the hardest of all relationships is perhaps all we have left to save: one with self.

I pray these words give their readers, therefore, what they gave me: hope to those who need it—comfort to those desperately needing to feel understood—courage to those needing reminded of the power of faith— and awareness to those who like me, never knew how easy it was to find yourself in a situation you'd never expect to be in. And when those seasons in our life come that strip us of our last, I hope this book reassures you of the growth that is coming in your life that you might not be able to see yet.

This book of poems is a recording of a mere season of my life. It was a season necessary before I could grow into the next. But most importantly, it was a season that I prayed for a long time, God would eventually bear His fruit in my life if I promised to remain rooted in Him. This book, therefore, blossomed out of His faithfulness. I have no idea what season of life you may find yourself in—what uncertainty you may be feeling, what pain you may be harboring, what you are struggling to let go of. I also don't know how these words might connect with you or if they will at all, but what I do know is that there is always something bigger at work. And so I pray that these words find the hands that need them.

Like naked trees rooted barefoot in the very earth, we are all capable of resilient strength despite our fragility. And through brave vulnerability, it is my hope that *The Seasons Reside in the Trees* will be a gift to its readers— connecting us all through our own individual seasons in life, with the possibility of what can blossom from the spaces we least expect.

A Photograph of the Sun (Self-Portrait)

I look like that.
Light leaking through a lens like
these glaring gutters smoke   the tips of my toes.
And suddenly the bike lane   turns my hands into hooves. I am serious.
Can you imagine   how that looks? My skin becomes distorted on canvas.
I lean   I bend   I throw my head   like a horse in a hackamore
in the wind.
I am a sunflower in coveralls   ask anyone.
I blur   my blare   my beauty shows into a terrible experience though.
I taste turquoise   it makes my toes pucker.   Yes
it would sound that strange   like pigment flinging its flicker   like
that bright.
It would be   surrendering to the experience   rather than trying to
put edges on the sun.

It's You

> *"A serious moment for the match is when it bursts into flame*
> *And is all alone, living in that instant, that beautiful second for which*
> *it was made."*   —Kenneth Koch

You're the match thrown on a propane tank.
You're the cigarette and you're the burn,
my dream that turned into smoke and
it's always been me who goes up in flames.

You are the machine that ate my damn quarter.
And I'll be the next whiskey you promised you wouldn't throw down.
Dirt clinging to the back of your jacket when we fall.
The cowlick I neither can control nor tame.

You are the promise to myself that if I could just heal,
I'd never forget to not put my hands back on the stove.
But with no odds to beat the rest, you are the loophole
my fingertips seek out of their own recklessness.

You're the hurricane of words and
when they drop I'll always be the rain.
My long lashes blinking like hazards.
It's you.

You're the crush that turned into a man.
You're the last time that's already had its past,
the second chance that ends back at the last,
and you're always what I'll never get back.

You are a full moon that haunts me in my sleep.
Midnight that will shatter from those trees.
The train and the sound of speed upon its tracks.
And I'll be what is left standing in nothing but bark.

You are the highway I drive upon straight into a funnel cloud.
The ice that gets into my veins and makes me shake.
The seasons in the trees and we are the coming back
to the one we'd almost thought we'd never again see.

You are my avant-garde,
the catastrophe Pollock left.
The ending I never saw coming
but leaves me thinking for days.

Love Poem that Ends in Apocalypse

I tried to say "don't leave me"
but instead a door flew out of my mouth.

I've always meant to tell you
I neither was expecting the magazines

we kept getting in the mail
I never subscribed to begin with, honey,

I told you it raining blueberries wasn't a good sign.
I told you one day those trees would hurt us,

it's something more you hear about these days.
What I meant to say is

watch out for the epoxy
setting us traps we'll remain stuck in.

I'm telling you now,
we weren't what the world was expecting.

Class Discussion

> "Later that night I held an atlas in my lap, ran my fingers across the whole world and whispered, where does it hurt? It answered: everywhere, everywhere, everywhere." —Warsan Shire

To the young girl in English class:
I want to gather you in my arms like air,
I want to protect you—I want to be your mother,
tell you to not make the same mistakes I once did.
But how do you hold onto a teenage girl without breaking her?

The world is constructed around telephone poles
stuck in the ground like thumb tacks
with strings running across a map:
we are all trying to get somewhere
or keep from finding the place we're at.

Oh darling, I see the marks upon your skin.
I see how you hold yourself.
I'm talking about the hammer
we use to fix things that gets
at our very thumbs.
The broken things that break us,
the wallpaper we use to surround a crumbing heart.

I'm talking about the brokenness behind your beautiful brown eyes.
I'm talking about what you are hiding behind those long sleeves.
And I want you to see I'm here now:
and I'll still be here
when the voice across the wires falls off of those trees.

One Cannot Bargain for a True Gift

It kills me saying goodbye to the leaves in the fall.
Your eyes have always alluded me:
the most arbitrary of color,
I will never identify.

Time feels like pinecones between us.
The air is cooling between our breaths,
things are getting crunchy.
There is this sinkhole we keep falling into,
the black hole you like to escape to
and leave me floating with no gravity.

The moon comes and it goes
with the ocean shadowing behind,
trying to peer over his shoulder
to see where on earth he is going.

Tears must be the body's way of flushing out the things we can't let go of.
And once again my heart is melting from my eyes,
and I have turned into water.

It's not the trees' fault they keep losing their leaves.
I would know, honey, I lost you the first time.
And leaf after leaf, leave after leave,
I became a bare trunk.

Our lives have been a Rubik's Cube.
But baby once the color in your eyes finally lines up,
you throw us right back into the game
and I'm not sure how many times I can rise from the ashes
without something still not left lying there.

I have fallen for you,
fallen at a trajectory of high speeds
racing the soles of your moving feet,
but honey, I am made of more than mere photosynthesis.

I have loved you centuries, it seems.
But I will never be that girl
and I think we both know
you will never be that man.

And when they ask me the color darkening again your eyes,
it kills me I will never have the answer.

gravitational pull

leaves are falling like pepper and
sliding across the ground
sounding like a snake's rattle

the wind's pallet is scratching echoes and
scraping messy reds and clunky yellows
upon the pavement's canvas

people want to hold onto things that are beautiful
I'd like to pluck the iridescence hanging upon your trees but
you just keep letting go peppering the ground with rattlesnakes

leaves are falling and illuminated like fireflies
but once their glow is only but a crunch upon the ground
those branches seem so lonely almost ugly

scary is empty
when you're no longer holding vibrant reds
and feeling the fire of yellow in your life

naked branches are standing in lost pigment
and I am
nothing but bark

A Eulogy for the Baby Bird that Cared

The trees have branches   they are cracking the sky.
When will those twigs and the light turn
green   both   silent as my lashes blinking.
I thought I could hold onto you   with my taloned toes
instead I hear my crunch   beneath your feet.

I knocked off a baby bird's nest
trying to hug your branch.
I cry for the unfortunate bystander   so that I don't feel so guilty
or responsible   because they will probably care   like me.

There are tree rings circling my fingertips
a bird's nest in my hair
on top of my head I am spinning
like the bottle   that pointed to you.

But now   all that tree is doing is staring at the thing on my face.
It is   so embarrassing.
I forgot to put on my oven mitts before kissing the stove.

Your penny knows to land on heads   so I'll pick you back up.
I look into Abraham Lincoln's disapproving stare
swimming in a pool of pennies   laughing at my luck.

It is   so   embarrassing.
I am a tree standing in nothing but bark.

This is the last time I'll let you leave me.
My baby bird is no longer waiting for you in its nest.
There is no nest.
I am no longer a baby bird.

It is raining in my shower.
I am holding the lost pieces in my hair.
It is raining in my shower.
Hurry   away
green means go.

haunted

knocky knock.   squiggle squirm phantom limb
there you are again   even after gone
curling my toes like a bladder full for too long
thorning my stomach   even after emptied feels wrong

I need to release you   or at least read you
but your eyes   are coarse braille
knocky knocky. like hail
and decentered neurons
hauntingly linger   an amputated limb
awakening inside me   like rattlesnakes
unfrozen   quakes and
leaping in my throat   cupsandcakes
in an elevator   too full
makes my stomach drop and just won't stop

a soul spitting   from salt shrieking eyes
a beaver's whoopsy flood   of dammed words
I amputated you   and now you're my missing limb
and there's that throat thing   again
like getting up too fast   hazards blinking like lashes
heart bang   it makes no sense
a vein interstating   caffeine shaking
a hallucinating presence   and dizzy absence

knock knock.
you're here

The Nature of Our Wrongs

In my head it all seems so clear now:
the sparrow singing from top of that tin roof,
the grass begging back for the grubs in their ground,
the dream on the wrong side of a Russian Roulette.

There were signs everywhere:
clouds sprawled out on the lawn,
tree roots thirsty in the sky.
Like trying to climb a rock pile,
each step forward left the rest falling behind.
We tried to climb even then into that blue
but instead only became the rain.

In one desperate attempt,
you tried to count,
and I tried to close my eyes.
I pulled the trap door,
but a way out there was none.

It all happened rather simply, really:
you—gripping onto bottles
we both knew were sharper than you let on;
me—rewalking that house like a ghost trying
to be released from whatever was binding it there.

Yet what I'll never understand
was why you kept telling me there wasn't a problem
with how you held onto the pebbles falling at our heads.
Like old combat buddies,
there was an inexplicable bond we couldn't rid ourselves of.

There was spaghetti sauce on the ceiling,
rust slowing down the kitchen clock
and crickets and cicadas whispering,
like broken chords mourning their own funeral.
Because it isn't life that I'm scared of,
it's the dying I can't live with.
And I've lived a thousand lives, it seems, just to be rebuilt.

Yes, there were signs everywhere:
the weeds together we pulled that kept growing again,
the storm one thinks they have finally waged
that backs up and hits with more speed.

What Remains Between Us

After the storm, we tried to pick up the broken glass
without letting it cut our already broken branches.
"If we can just make it through this season,"
I keep telling the leaves falling from my hands.
"If you can just keep holding on," I try to reason with myself.

You and I scrubbed the floor and threw away in the trash
the things we knew we could never get rid of, and yet
I know you know that what lies broken between us has already
fallen from our fingers, nor can no longer be pieced back.
"If we can just keep holding on," I plead cradling you in my chest.

Petals remained upon the pavement: Sunflowers slowing losing their sun.
Think about clothes that always slide off the hanger,
ice disappearing in the glass of your whiskey.
We are always trying to get rid of or keep from losing things,
hoping we're not on the disposable end.

We want the piggy bank back before it broke,
before anyone was permitted to gather what was inside,
the clouds before the rain,
the leaves before the trees,
the colors before the bark.

I Hide It Surprisingly Well

Below bath water and bubbles on my left knee,
there will always be a scar I'll remember you and my fragility by.

I've tried not to think about the shattered glass,
the lamp hunched over leaning
like our backs hovering to the ground in the aftermath.

The liquor I poured out the front door
you made me get down on my hands and knees to scrub,
rain blurring the edges of the house we once called our home.

That scar upon my knee still occasionally burns red
thinking about the moment I looked down
to what your pavement took from me,
the life I haven't been able to regenerate,
because there's no breaking our kind of fall.

The Poem without Forgiveness
Inspired by Dean Young

You want to be taken back after behaving terribly
but nothing can be taken back,
not the ashes from the fire, the trees from the leaves,
the crumbs of your love, the damage from the smoke.
You want to take back the ugly things you did, and I said,
but nothing can be taken back—not you, not
pink picked off fingernail polish lying in the sheets of a bed.
The heart hoards its gunk
just as the living hoard their junk.
Something inside of me will always hold onto you,
emptied handed yet still unwilling to let go.
I've laid my face on your pavement,
slammed my fingers into its stone,
pulled on your coattails begging you not to go.
You left me alone burning without you in our bed
but when you got back you still weren't even there.
Nothing can be taken back,
not that ring, not even that dress.
You want to be the man who has me back,
but nothing can be taken back—not those lies,
not the velocity of the rollercoaster, not its havoc.
You want it all back
but we've already tried that.
Pounding on my door,
it is your body hiccupping in shame, now,
your nose dripping with snot pleading to the floor.
But my love, nothing can be taken back, not years, not our luck.
The heart hoards its gunk.

Just because you've done too much doesn't mean I wanted it all;
just because I've had enough doesn't mean you meant too much.

Taking on the Sun

Every morning I race the sun
so that I have time to whisper to the stars before the sun scares them all
under the hill,
though lately I have been questioning everything.

It is said that the sun has a split personality—one to rise, one to set.
I read somewhere this is normal,
though lately I have been questioning everything.

Take the washing machine,
take us, for example, we are cycling to new phases
every morning racing the sun.

Half the moon has been ripped away—trimmed with toenail clippers,
It doesn't really matter which, just that without you,
it and I have been questioning everything.

The secrets you tucked away roll out of the drawers we can't keep shut.
Someone told me once that chlorax can remove just about any stain,
though lately I have been questioning everything.

These memories have sharp edges
I keep getting caught on like panty hose would,
every morning with small snags running down my side
because lately, I have been questioning everything.

The Epoxy of Our Pasts

I didn't expect the birds
nor the shit I threw
before flapping you away.
Years are wound around us like tree rings,
like barbed wire around the bark
we keep getting tangled back in.
Oh, the train is taking off
its wheels spinning
and the smoke building,
my heart is as anxious as that whistle
piercing through the very air we use to breathe.
Please don't jump back on, please,
those tracks are a trap
that over the high bridge above the creek
no longer with wings
they disappear and drop.

Hope Is a Dammed Thing

I just wanted you to know that I still have the butterfly figurine
I put in your bag you took during treatment to keep you strong
once you gave back to me your own darkest cocoon.

I've tried not to think about the night
you broke down my door while I was sleeping,
nor the stranger I woke up to that looked like you.
I didn't have time to tell you,
but I'm not sure how the bottle you threw at the wall didn't break.

Slow down the roll of film, picture the words
out of your mouth shaped into letters.
Now, picture me as that bottle.
I'm still not sure how I didn't break.

It only takes a moment to blow the seeds off the dandelion, a star to fall,
the caterpillar pleading against its own silk,
what mere ice can do to an entire glass, one altered substance to another.

It's terrible, what adrenaline does to the eye:
when all along we can't even see what is right in front of us.
When you left,
I didn't recognize the plates that had shifted inside of me
the way my hands had turned into little quakes,
the acid rain you'd spit me back out as,
the chew you purposefully left glazed on the corners of my sink.

And I didn't tell you, but the last time I saw you
there was a look in your eyes that reminded me
of a phantom, a thief, a child trying to decide if
he should tell what he senses his mother already knows.

When two blue claw crabs are put into a bucket,
both become enmeshed reaching towards the light,
two individuals trying to climb on the same sinking life boat,
alchemy that attracted the wrong atom,
the egg inside the wrong yoke,
the heart that forgot it was made of gold.

I just wanted you to know that I still have that old thing,
that mysterious creature of hope balled up in my heart,
the person I know inside of you softer than skin of velvet,
flapping its wings pleading to be let out,
threatening to take off with me again.

We Would Be Aligned with the Universe Again

Somewhere, in some galaxy, maybe light years away,
there is a family of possibilities, with us in them.

We're a fundamental equation, baby,
with a solution the universe never predicted.

Take an operational definition
operating free will to every organism

but add quantum mechanics, honey
and an element of randomness is added in.

Our brains contain a hundred million, billion, billion particles,
leaving a lot of room for quantum chaos, an occasional fuckup.

Take you
take me

operating in operational routines,
you on the right side of the bed, and I on the left,

with my head tucked gently into your chest.
My love, it only took one small unexpected choice,

it only took one choice unnatural to our human behavior,
one element of quantum chaos to extinguish our happy-ever-after.

Maybe if we could just self-reference,
if we could just time travel,

if we could just swap the family of possibilities we ended up in
maybe light years away in some galaxy, baby universe, or black hole

we could go back to the possibility of us,
the possibility of what the universe previously determined.

The Poem that Knows Something

Rome lies in rubbles,
what we once loved
has crumbled before our very eyes.

We overcame goblins and gothic eras
and ghosts in the night.
We have traveled moon beams, ocean waves,
and through alleyways we've squeezed.

We jumped through windows with balconies below,
swung from ceilings and balanced on tips of cathedrals.
Gladiator fights pounded the coliseum,
foot after foot,
generation from every side of the earth,
stomping their prints like stamps upon our dirt.
Yet, our two trembling pillars bravely held the city up.

There are rarely settling endings to memorable stories,
and neither did we have the happy ending
I ever was so after.

There is a history about us, my love,
it's the part that repeats itself
we forgot again was coming.

Worlds Away

I have been the girl with blue petals in my eyes,
always falling for you,
soft as water strong as the ocean,
made of the very things that tear
our horizon apart. But the moon,
it took you away and then
slid you back into my hands,
like two fingers clasped,
like the sun makes the moon
finally look full again, but the cigarette smoke
keeps covering up its man and his smile.
I am begging for my ship to gather
you in my arms, like hope, like that of land.
When I left there were tears in your eyes
building and welling like tides,
pulling you in and pulling you back out,
and there was something about the dizzy
I felt when you looked away that left me
alone again, like that man
packing his cigarettes, and the smoke
behind this boat billowing away.

Just Keep Walking
Dedicated to Beverly

I have been contemplating
how to piece back to myself
the branches in my arms
I could no longer hold onto.

And I have been waiting, patiently,
to know what to do
with what now remains at my feet.

Yet, in the faint glimpses of myself
in the renewal of morning light,
I kneel quietly before my bed in prayer.
It is no longer someone else's hand I am reaching for.

These hands I fold together feel suddenly so small
next to a peace now holding onto me.
It is in these moments
I have discovered what was there all along.

And so in a new quiet strength,
I give myself permission
to keep up with my lungs and beating chest
as I find my feet,
and let them move me forward.

The Nature of the Beast

Somewhere
at some point
we all must lose everything
and everyone we love.

Earth is such an uncanny place.
Yet, still
we unpack our roots
and stretch out their arms into its soil
letting people fly in and out of our very branches.

Trees must be the kindest of creatures
reaching for the sun
open branches dancing in the light
sniffing another's hands like a horse
before offering them their leaves.

Sometimes I wonder why I even let myself love
when those shadows will at some point gallop away.
But then
I run my hands across grains protecting a substance
bigger than its mere bark.
A season is coming it hasn't yet seen.

writing at dawn

there is this photo-
synthesis. your light
in my own little veins.
and it wilds my wings.

I'd spit on my fists
punch a lion in
the nose. not to hurt
him though. because I

I have to burst. I
mean I have a new
chemical energy.
what I'm saying is

I'm into explosives.
like waning moonlight
being eaten by
giggling porcupines.

how sweet, right? like the
surprise a kernel makes
when it realizes
it can pop without

destroying. like snow-
flakes falling without a cloud in
sight. the horizon sparks chlorophyll.
I look into it, I absorb your light.

What I Want You to Know

Wasn't life so much easier when our biggest worry
was just about as big as our size four shoe. Now
we close the journal that exposes our insides and
hope someone will be able to read it anyway.
Anyway,
its pages are closed
like the secret that wants to be told like
the time at the tea party when I
reserved a special chair for my stuffed animal
who I never told and who never showed up
but I wanted to know.
I am finding my old shoes in my closet
that looked like alligators or dandelions
or a snapping flower with yellow bark.
And yet
I still stick my hand into the dark
feeling around to find them just
so that I can cover my feet.
Last night I dreamed I ended up in Costa Rica.
"Make sure to attach your safety mask
before helping anyone else with theirs,"
the flight attendant said over the intercom.
I suppose we have to save ourselves
before we can anyone else.

The Seasons Reside in the Trees
> *"Abide in me, and I in you. The branch cannot bear fruit unless you remain in me."* —John 15:4

When the smoke cleared,
there was this heart beating,
just beating down in the dirt.

Can you believe that?
Just opening and closing
to open again,
all for the reason to close.

And then I realized
the way it was guarding itself
from its very own chest,
lying there sprawled out in the dirt
getting grains in veins of
a small and abandoned heart.

And so I gently knelt down
and as to not scare it I softly whispered in its ear:
"Don't ever mistake the branches you had to prune
for missing parts—never mistake healing
for a final destination—nor lessons for baggage, my love.

If there is one person you can trust, it's you.
If there's one person you should choose, it's you.
You can finally love, without losing yourself.
You can say what you need now,
you've had what it takes to take care of yourself all along."

And it looked up at me, unsure,
still questioning itself.
So I reached down
smoothing away the leaves from its eyes I smiled:

"Letting go is not failure,
ask the leaves as they challenge the wind,
ask the seasons in the trees.
Instead let the life they've regenerated
bloom out of your hands
and become a gift to you and to others."

Quietly it smiled back at me,
and so picking it off the ground,
I gently put it back where it belonged.

Taylor Tessa Lutz fell in love with writing at a young age. When asked in first grade what she wanted to be when she grew up, Taylor drew an author. She is now an English Language Arts teacher trying to plant seeds to inspire other young budding writers in the world.

During her undergraduate she became active in the writing department at Nebraska Wesleyan University. After being exposed to more abstract forms of art, Taylor soon became inspired by nature, surrealism, and a juxtaposition of imagery. Working with her poetry professor on a grant, she received a scholarship to attend the Juniper Writing Institute.

At Nebraska Wesleyan University Lutz received the Boatright Award in Poetry. Nine poems as well as two short stories were published in their student-run publication, the *Flintlock*. She became the co-editor of poetry for the *Flintlock* during her undergraduate and helped online as a visiting editor for *The Penmen Review* while completing her Master's in English and Creative Writing and Poetry at Southern New Hampshire University. Her work has recently been featured in *The Paddock Review*.

She believes that coffee, laughter, random acts of kindness, and leather journals with textured paper are quite possibly some of the greatest luxuries in life. Taylor grew up on a farm and ranch in rural Nebraska and therefore also has a love for the expansive terrain and open skies of the Midwest. Taylor's owes everything to her family, loved ones, and strong faith.

www.ingramcontent.com/pod-product-compliance
Lightning Source LLC
LaVergne TN
LVHW041509070426
835507LV00012B/1443